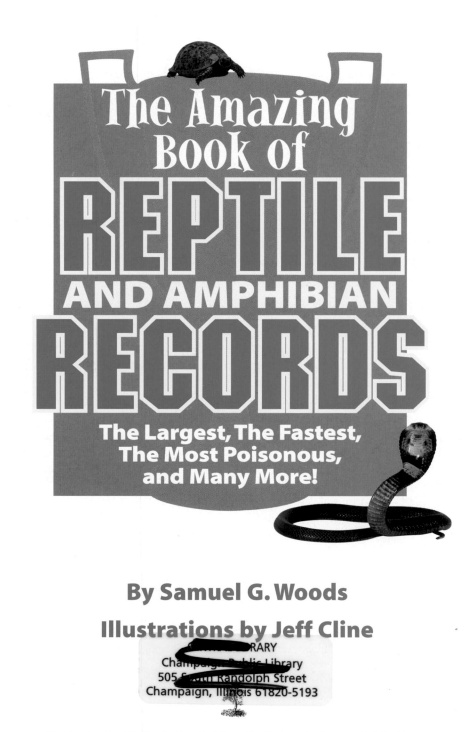

The Amazing Book of REPTILE AND AMPHIBIAN RECORDS

The Largest, The Fastest, The Most Poisonous, and Many More!

By Samuel G. Woods

Illustrations by Jeff Cline

BLACKBIRCH PRESS, INC.

WOODBRIDGE, CONNECTICUT

Published by Blackbirch Press, Inc.
260 Amity Road
Woodbridge, CT 06525
web site: http://www.blackbirch.com
e-mail: staff@blackbirch.com

© 2000 Blackbirch Press, Inc.
First Edition

Printed in China

10 9 8 7 6 5 4 3 2 1

Photo Credits
Cover: (Clockwise from top left corner) lizard: ©PhotoDisc; snake: ©Photo Spin; lizard: ©Photo Spin; frog: ©Photo Spin; turtle: ©PhotoDisc; lizard: ©Photo Spin; frog: ©PhotoDisc; snake, lizard, snake: ©Photo Spin; lizard: ©PhotoDisc; frog, turtle, alligator, frog: ©Photo Spin; snake, frog, snake: ©PhotoDisc; lizard: ©Photo Spin; turtle, frog: ©PhotoDisc; snake: ©Photo Spin; lizard, turtle: ©PhotoDisc; title page and table of contents: PhotoDisc; page 5: ©Jeffery Rotham/Peter Arnold; pages 7,17: ©James Gerholdt; pages 8, 9, 14, 15: ©Corel Corporation; page 11: ©Compost/Visage/Peter Arnold; page 13: ©Dr. Paul Zahl/Photo Researchers; page 19: ©Secret Sea Visions/Peter Arnold; page 21: ©Fritz Prenzel/Animals Animals; page 23: ©Roland Seitre/Peter Arnold; page 25: ©Joe McDonald/Corbis; pages 27, 31: ©Kevin Schafer/Peter Arnold; page 29: ©Heinz Plenge/Peter Arnold.

Library of Congress Cataloging-in-Publication Data
Woods, Samuel G.
   The amazing book of reptile and amphibian records: the largest, the fastest, the longest-lived, and many more! / by Samuel G. Woods; illustrations by Jeff Cline.
      p. cm.
   Includes bibliographical references (p.) and index.
   Summary: Introduces, in question and answer format, such record-breaking amphibians and reptiles as the chameleon, reticulated python, Galapagos giant tortoise, and poison arrow frog.
      ISBN 1-56711-368-0
      1. Reptiles—Miscellanea—Juvenile literature. 2. Amphibians—Miscellanea—Juvenile literature. [1. Reptiles—Miscellanea. 2. Amphibians—Miscellanea. 3. Questions and answers.]
I. Cline, Jeff, ill. II. Title
QL644.2.W66 2000   99–042522
597.9—dc21   CIP

Contents

What's the LARGEST Reptile?

The Saltwater Crocodile

These crocs can reach up to 26 feet (7.9 m) in length and can weigh more than 2,200 pounds (998 kg)!

Saltwater crocodiles can travel great distances in the ocean.

NOTEPAD

The world's largest reptiles are found in Asia, near the islands of the South Pacific, and in Australia. They are excellent swimmers, and have been known to travel great distances by sea. Unfortunately, these huge creatures are valued highly for their hides. The skin of a saltwater croc is the most expensive in the world.

NOTEWORTHY: Saltwater crocodile young are actually raised in fresh water. When the crocklet has grown, it is pushed into a salt water environment by an adult.

Which Reptile Has the MOST UNIQUE EYES?

The Chameleon

Chameleons are the only reptiles that can move each eye independently! They can focus together (like human eyes) to see in three dimensions, or they can focus separately on two different objects at the same time!

NOTEPAD

Chameleons are very unique reptiles in many ways. In addition to their special eyes, they also have the longest relative tongues of any reptile. A chameleon's tongue can be as long as its entire body! It also has an incredible ability to change color. A chameleon will change color to hide itself, or sometimes to reflect its mood!

Chameleons can change color for camouflage or to reflect their moods.

What's the FASTEST LIZARD?

The Spiny-tailed Iguana

This scaly, long-tailed creature can run up to 22 miles (35 km) per hour!

NOTEPAD

Spiny-tailed iguanas are found mostly in Mexico and Central America. They are relatively small lizards, on average growing between 24–36 inches (61–91 cm) in length. These iguanas are very unfriendly toward humans and prefer to live in groups where one male is the designated leader.

Spiny-tailed iguanas are relatively small lizards.

What's the LONGEST SNAKE?

• • • • • • • •

The Reticulated Python

This huge snake can reach lengths of more than 35 feet (10.7 m)! That's about the length of the average school bus!

. . . .
Reticulated pythons can weigh up to 300 pounds (136 kg).

NOTEPAD

An average reticulated python weighs about 300 pounds (136 kg) and can live up to 20 years in captivity (cared for by humans). Pythons are not venemous. Instead, they kill their prey by strangulation. Once a python has wrapped its huge body around an animal, it will constrict (tighten) its muscles and squeeze so hard that the prey cannot breathe.

What's the LARGEST FROG?

The Goliath Frog

This frog weighs about 7 pounds (3 kg) and measures about 3 feet (1 m) in length. Fully grown, it is the same size as a baby deer!

Goliath frogs have huge webbed feet, which makes them powerful swimmers.

NOTEPAD

Goliath frogs are found in west central Africa. Scientists did not even know this species of frog existed before 1906. It was then that they were discovered by scientists in the jungle. With huge webbed feet, these amphibians are powerful swimmers.

NOTEWORTHY: Goliath frogs are currently endangered because their rain forest habitats are being destroyed so quickly by humans.

13

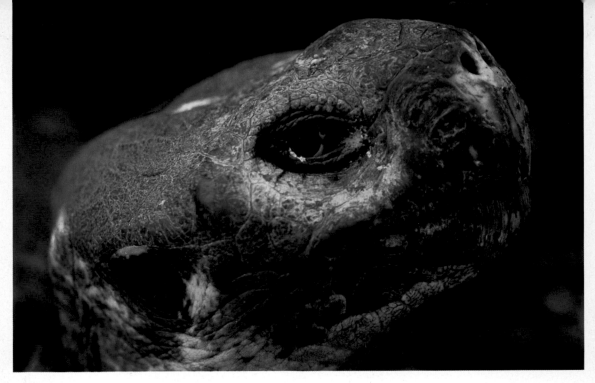

What's the LONGEST-LIVED Reptile?

The Galapagos Giant Tortoise

Some of these tortoises have been known to live 150 years!

NOTEPAD

These giant reptiles do everything slowly. They move slowly. They eat slowly. And, even though they can weigh up to 500 pounds (226 kg), they can go without eating or drinking for weeks. When they do eat, it can take them up to 3 weeks to digest their food!

NOTEWORTHY: Galapagos tortoises are an endangered species. Less than 15,000 are alive today.

....
Galapagos tortoises are long lived but are in danger of becoming extinct.

What's the MOST POISONOUS Amphibian?

The Poison Arrow Frog

The most dangerous poison arrow frog has enough poison in its skin to kill 20 adult humans!

NOTEPAD

Poison arrow frogs are also known as poison dart frogs. They got their name as the result of how they are used. South American Indians coat their arrowheads with the poison from the skins of these frogs before hunting. There are more than 50 known species of these highly toxic amphibians. Most poison arrow frogs are brightly colored. Scientists believe the bright colors are meant to warn potential enemies to stay away.

The bright coloring of many poison arrow frogs warns other animals to stay away.

What's the MOST POISONOUS SNAKE?

The Sea Snake

All sea snakes are venemous. One sea snake, found in a reef off the northern coast of Australia, has a poison that is 100 times more toxic than any land snake!

This banded sea snake is one of the ocean's deadliest swimmers.

NOTEPAD

Sea snakes are not only very dangerous, they are also excellent swimmers. Many can stay underwater for up to 5 hours at a time. About 70 different species of sea snakes live in the world's oceans. Most are found in warmer waters, particularly in the Pacific and Indian oceans, the Bay of Bengal, and the Persian Gulf.

What's the MOST POISONOUS LAND SNAKE?

The Fierce Snake

Less than 4/1000 of an ounce of this snake's poison can kill about 250,000 mice!

Fierce snakes are also called small-scaled snakes or inland taipans.

NOTEPAD

This snake is also called the small-scaled snake or the inland taipan. It is found mostly in central Australia. This dangerous reptile can grow to more than 8 feet (2.5 m) long. Unlike its larger cousins—the vipers—fierce snakes have fixed fangs instead of retractable ones (that move in and out). That means they are unable to sink their fangs into skin once their mouths are closed.

What's the LARGEST LIZARD?

The Komodo Dragon

These monsters grow up to 10 feet (3 m) long and can weigh up to 230 pounds (104 kg). An adult komodo can eat an entire deer in one sitting!

A komodo dragon can eat half its body weight in 20 minutes.

NOTEPAD

These large lizards are huge eaters. They are able to eat half their body weight in 20 minutes. In one meal, they are able to consume 80% of their body weight. After eating so much, a komodo will often sleep for up to a week while it digests its meal! More than 50 different bacteria can be found in the saliva of a komodo dragon. At least seven of those bacteria are quite poisonous.

Which SNAKE has the LONGEST FANGS?

Gaboon vipers are the largest snakes in the viper family.

The Gaboon Viper

This large snake has fangs that can extend more than 2 inches (5 cm)!

The Gaboon viper is the largest of all the snakes in the viper family. A full-grown adult averages about 6 feet (1.8 m) in length and can weigh up to 25 pounds (11 kg). These reptiles spend much of their time hiding in piles of leaves, waiting to surprise unsuspecting rodents, birds, or frogs.

What's the LARGEST TURTLE?

The Pacific Leatherback

The largest leatherback ever recorded weighed more than 2,000 pounds (915 kg) and was more than 8 feet (2 m) long!

These are the largest living species of turtle. Because of their size, leatherbacks eat an incredible amount of food, particularly jellyfish. Young leatherbacks have been known to eat twice their weight in jellyfish every day! Even the most poisonous jellyfish (lion's mane and Portuguese man-o-war) don't bother these hungry reptiles.

NOTEWORTHY: Pacific leatherbacks also hold the record for fastest reptiles in water. They can swim up to 22 miles (35 km) per hour.

What's the HEAVIEST SNAKE?

The Anaconda

A full-grown anaconda can weigh 500 pounds (227 kg) and measure 44 inches (112 cm) around. That's almost 4 feet (1.8 m) around—thicker than most 20- or 30-year-old tree trunks!

NOTEPAD

These huge reptiles are members of the boa family. Although their bite is severe, they are not venemous. Found mostly in Central and South America, these snakes spend most of their time in the water. Some anacondas grow as long as 33 feet (10 m) and can live up to 30 years, which is possibly the record for snakes.

Anacondas are not only long and heavy, they are also long lived.

What's the MOST ANCIENT Reptile?

• • • • • • • •

The Tuatara

This ancient species of reptile was living on Earth millions of years before the dinosaurs! It is the only living member of a group of reptiles called "beak heads."

Tuataras are the only reptiles with three eyes (though the third is only visible in the young).

NOTEPAD

Tuataras are found only on islands off the coast of New Zealand. These small reptiles have many unique features. The crests on their necks are made from special cells that raise up when the animal is alarmed. They also have tails that can break off and then grow back! And tuataras actually have three eyes! The third eye is usually only visible in the young, and scientists don't think it really functions.

Glossary

Bacteria—microscopic life forms that live all around and inside us. Many bacteria are good, but some are dangerous.

Captivity—cared for by humans.

Dimension—the measurement or size of an object. All objects have three dimensions: length, width, and height.

Endangered species—an animal that is in danger of extinction, or dying out.

Hide—the skin of an animal that is used for a human purpose.

Reef—a strip of rock, sand, or coral close to the surface of a body of water.

Retractable—able to be moved or pulled back.

Saliva—fluid inside the mouth that helps an animal swallow and begin digestion.

Severe—painful or dangerous.

Toxic—poisonous.

Venemous—poisonous.

Viper—a family of poisonous snakes.

For More Information

Books

Howell, Catherine. *Reptiles and Amphibians* (Nature Library). Washington, D.C.: National Geographic, 1993.

Martin, James. Art Wolfe (Photographer). *Frogs*. New York, NY: Crown Publications, 1997.

Pipe, Jim. *The Giant Book of Snakes and Slithery Creatures* (Giant Book Of). Brookfield, CT: Copper Beech Books, 1998.

Ricciuti, Edward. Vincent Marteka (Editor). *Amphibians* (Our Living World). Woodbridge, CT: Blackbirch Press, Inc., 1994.

Web Sites

NOVA Crocodiles
Learn about the 23 different species of crocodiles—www.pbs.org/wgbh/nova/crocs

Turtle Trax
This kid's page explains the dangers that sea turtles face and how humans can help—www.turtles.org/kids.htm

Index